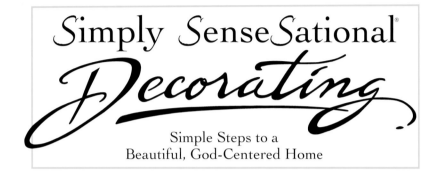

Simply SenseSational®
Decorating

Simple Steps to a
Beautiful, God-Centered Home

TERRY WILLITS

with photographs by Tim Olive

ZondervanPublishingHouse
Grand Rapids, Michigan

A Division of HarperCollinsPublishers

Simply SenseSational® Decorating
Text copyright © 2000 by Terry Willits
Photographs copyright © 2000 by Tim Olive

Requests for information should be addressed to:

 ZondervanPublishingHouse
Grand Rapids, Michigan 49530

Library of Congress Cataloging-in-Publication Data

Willits, Terry, 1959-
    Simply SenseSational decorating : simple steps to a beautiful, God-centered home / Terry Willits ; with photographs by Tim Olive.
       p. cm.
    ISBN 0-310-22891-3 (hc)
    1. House furnishings. 2. Interior decoration. I. Title.
TX311 .W537 2000
645—dc21   99-086297
                                                               CIP

This edition printed on acid-free paper.

Interior design by Amy E. Langeler

Printed in Singapore

00 01 02 03 04 05 06 /❖ TWP/ 10 9 8 7 6 5 4 3 2 1

Beautiful homes grow from the inside out.

To Sandra Johnson,
whose beautiful home simply mirrors her heart.
Thanks for your encouragement over the years.

Contents

INTRODUCTION 6

STARTING SIMPLY 13

Simply Dreaming 15
Simply Scheming 24

Section 1

Section 2

FORMING THE FRAMEWORK 37

Simply Floors 39
Simply Walls 54

Section 3

FILLING YOUR HOME 73
Simply Furniture 75
Simply Windows 96
Simply Accessories 116
A Simply SenseSational Home 132

Introduction

I have a confession. For a long time, I struggled with being an interior designer. Don't get me wrong, I love decorating, especially my own home. As a woman, I love bringing color and comfort, life and love into the walls that surround my family. I have fun feathering my nest with beautiful fabrics, fluffy pillows, cozy rugs, pretty pictures, and more. And as an interior designer, I enjoy helping others bring beauty into their own corners of the world.

My struggle was that I knew in the big picture of life, material things don't really matter. When we leave our earthly homes someday, we won't be taking anything with us, no matter how beautiful. So, as an interior designer, I asked myself, "Am I just wasting my time helping people with materialistic stuff, or is there something of lasting value in this profession?"

Digging into God's Word, I found my answer. Beauty not only matters to our Creator, he is the author of it. In Genesis, God created beauty upon the earth, and the Garden of Eden became man's first home.

Our eternal home, heaven, is detailed symbolically in the book of Revelation (Chapter 21), giving us a peek inside a place so beautiful it will defy description.

Between Genesis and Revelation in the second book of Chronicles (chapter 3), we can read about God's earthly dwelling place. God cared about every minute detail in the building of his temple, and made sure it was decorated to his precise specifications.

Understanding that God is a God of beauty, order, and detail, I realized that while seeking beauty alone in our homes is hollow, there is nothing wrong with enhancing our own dwelling places in a balanced fashion — making sure we are worshiping God, not the "stuff."

The message of SenseSational Homes was born out of this discovery. I wanted others like myself — who might be discouraged or intimidated by picture-perfect decorator show houses or slick home magazine photographs — to be set free! I wanted to remind women there's more to a home than just how it looks. A truly beautiful home blossoms as relationships are celebrated and each of the five senses are stimulated in simple ways.

Over the years, I've written and spoken about how to create a SenseSational home. Women love this fresh and freeing approach of awakening the five senses to make a warm, friendly home; yet many ask, "When I do decorate and focus on the visual appeal of my home, where do I begin? How can I make my home look beautiful without breaking the bank? How do I develop a decorating plan?"

Simply SenseSational Decorating has been written to answer these very questions. Its purpose is to focus on the practical ABCs of decorating. The pages that follow use God's orderly steps for creating his beautiful world as a blueprint for

> He has made everything beautiful in its time. He has also set eternity in the hearts of men.
>
> **Ecclesiastes 3:11**

7

decorating our homes. *Simply SenseSational Decorating* is not an exhaustive encyclopedia covering every design element that exists; rather, it is a back-to-basics book intended to take the guesswork out of decorating and put the fun back in!

Before beginning to decorate your home, there are a few critical things for you to remember, and some equally important things you might need to forget.

Some things to remember . . .

You are the best decorator for your home

There is no one more qualified to decorate your home than you. It's true! God made you unique, and the only way for you to feel "at home" in your home is to express that uniqueness. But it's going to take some time to educate yourself about your tastes and personal style. Even if you hire a professional decorator to assist you with your home, her purpose should be to draw out your personal style, to guide you, and to assist you with resources. If you want your house to be *your* home, then *you* need to be involved!

Confidence is key

Confidence comes with knowledge and experience. The more you do anything, the easier it becomes! As you become educated about your decorating style and options, you'll feel more confident with your decisions, and enjoy decorating more.

> The more you do anything, the easier it becomes!

Go with Your Gut

When making selections, trust your instincts. Don't purchase anything you think will "grow" on you. Believe in love at first sight. If something appeals to you instantly, that's your personal style!

You Cannot Have Beauty Without Order

Disorder distracts the eye from being able to appreciate anything that is beautiful. Before you break out the paint roller or bring in more "stuff," you may need to clear some clutter so you can see the bones of your home.

People Are the Priority

Our motivation for decorating should simply be to create a beautiful place where people can come to be loved, refreshed, and encouraged. Check your priorities — do you get more upset over a broken glass or a broken heart?

A few things to forget . . .

Forget the "Rules"

The truth is, there are no decorating rules, only principles. Rules mean there are right ways and wrong ways to do things. It's your home, and you can decorate however you desire. If you are fearful of decorating, perhaps it's because of the mixed information you hear. "Use pairs." "Use threes." "Use a touch of black." "Use a splash of yellow." Decorating is subjective. If you hired five different decorators or asked five different friends for decorating advice, it's likely each would tell you something different.

There are, however, principles, or basic truths, in decorating. For example, dark colors make a room cozier and smaller; light colors make it appear larger. Throughout the book, I'll share simple suggestions and design principles that may help guide you. But don't feel obliged to follow anything. Decorate your home for you and your family, not anyone else!

> The first rule of decorating is to throw out all the rules!
>
> **Billy Baldwin**

FORGET THE FADS

The home decorating industry, like the fashion industry, has trends. Just because a certain chartreuse chenille fabric might be "in style" doesn't mean it should be part of your decorating scheme. Learn the latest resources that are available, but listen to your heart and your treasures will be timeless. I love yellow, whether it's rated by the design industry as the hottest color or not. No matter what the trends, my home will always have yellow.

> Listen to your heart and your treasures will be timeless.

FORGET PAST MISTAKES

If you bought a comforter on sale and now you really don't like it, don't decorate a whole room around it. Chalk it up to experience, but don't decorate around a disaster. You'll end up wasting more money on a room you didn't love from the start.

FORGET "KEEPING UP WITH THE JONESES"

Playing the comparison game is a sure way to steal your joy and contentment. No two homes are the same. Rather than focusing on what you don't have where you live, bloom where you are planted, and enjoy the treasures you do have.

FORGET ACHIEVING PERFECTION

There is no such thing as a perfect home on this side of heaven. Strive for quality, not perfection. If you're a perfectionist, loosen up a bit and you'll have more fun decorating.

Recognizing that a beautiful home is not an end in itself but a means to a greater end — creating a pleasant place that reflects God's love, beauty, and care — I offer this book to you. May the pages that follow help you gain confidence and joy as you decorate your home.

So snuggle up on your hand-me-down sofa, roll up your sleeves, and get ready as we begin our journey together to "simply decorate" your home.

Don't decorate around a disaster.

You shall not covet your neighbor's house.

Exodus 20:17

Starting Simply

Decorating can be fun and fulfilling when approached one step at a time.

1

*B*eautiful homes don't happen overnight. They evolve. Layer by layer. Choice by choice. Piece by piece. From dreaming about your home, to selecting that first fabric, to placing the finishing accessories, decorating is a journey. And the best way to begin a journey is to take just one simple step. Then another. And before you know it, you're getting somewhere.

Whether you're living in a brand-new home with all white walls, working on a "fixer upper," building your dream home, or moving into your very first apartment, decorating can be fun and fulfilling *when approached one step at a time*. If, however, you are trying to tackle your whole house from top to bottom with a tight deadline, decorating quickly becomes overwhelming and frustrating — far from what it should be.

Think about it. When God created the world, he didn't do it all in one day! So why should you expect yourself to create a beautiful home instantly? The key to simply decorating a beautiful home that reflects your personal style is to go slowly and enjoy the process.

So where do you begin? The first two steps to decorating simply are to take time to *dream* and then develop a *scheme*.

> When God created the world, he didn't do it all in one day.

Simply Dreaming

Dreaming is the first step towards reality. Dreaming doesn't cost you a dime and can actually save you money in the long run. Once you've spent time dreaming and discovering your decorating style, you will be better able to express yourself in the home you create.

Now is the time to open your eyes and observe. Do your homework. Be a student of yourself. Learn what you love. And dream — open your mind and your heart.

REMEMBER FAVORITE PLACES

Think about some of the favorite homes you've visited in the past. What appealed to you about them? What elements of those homes could you incorporate into your own home? I remember sinking into the comfy down sofa of a neighbor's home I often visited as a child. I also loved the home of my dear childhood friend, Jan, whose warm, inviting house was filled with yellow. Because of these memories, comfort and warmth are both qualities I want my home to have today.

> Comfort and warmth are qualities I want my home to have.

GO SHOPPING WITHOUT YOUR WALLET

Tour model homes in newly developed neighborhoods. Visit furniture show-rooms and decorator houses. Browse antique stores and specialty shops. Notice what you love. Educate yourself on quality and pricing. Ask questions. Take your camera and a dream notebook and document anything that inspires you.

In Atlanta, we have an annual event called "Street of Dreams," during which a whole neighborhood of decorator show houses is opened to the public to visit. What a place to go for inspiration! (My husband, Bill, jokingly refers to the event as the "Street of Nightmares" and the "Road to Discontentment.") One year, we walked into a bright, open home and immediately fell in love with its sunny, yellow walls. A brochure noted the color as a Duron paint color named "Sesame." I have used the same color for clients many times since.

REFLECT ON YOUR PERSONALITY

If someone walked into your home, what could they learn about you or your family? ("A lot!" you may be thinking with a chuckle.) Your home should reflect the personalities of those who live there. Think about the personalities of those who live under your roof. Maybe your overall look is daring and dramatic. Casual yet elegant. Clean and classic. Bright and cheerful. Rustic and natural.

PONDER YOUR PASSIONS

If you had a whole day to do whatever you wanted, where would you go, what would you do? Think about the things you and your family enjoy in life. The inside of your home should reflect what you like to do outside your home.

Do you prefer a nature walk to a tea party? Does your husband love a particular sport? Do you enjoy traveling? How can your walls whisper about the people who live there? Bill loves golf. Our house wouldn't be his home if it didn't express his passion somewhere. His hunter green office holds his golfing treasures — one of his grandfather's old golf clubs, photographs of admired golfers, special golf balls, trophies, and more.

> The inside of your home should reflect what you like to do outside your home.

CONSIDER YOUR FAVORITE COLORS

Take a walk outside and let nature's beauty inspire you. God, the Master Artist, has painted beautiful colors on his outdoor canvas. What colors delight you? Color influences mood more than any other visual element. Blue is soothing, peaceful, and cool. Yellow is energizing, hopeful, and cheerful. Red is passionate, intense, and powerful. Green is natural and calming. Black is timeless and sophisticated. White is clean and airy. What colors would you like to paint on your canvas?

I love the beach, where the warm gold of the sand meets the cool blue of the ocean. This setting was the starting point for decorating our master bedroom. Though we live far from the ocean, I wanted to recreate that same soothing feeling within the walls of our bedroom — and it all began with dreaming about what I love.

DREAM WITH A NOTEBOOK

If you're like me, a favorite little luxury in life is to find a beautiful home magazine, curl up in a cozy chair with a beverage in hand, and get lost in the pages. It's the perfect time to dream about my home!

For creative inspiration, start a dream notebook by collecting pictures from your favorite home magazines. Collecting pretty pictures doesn't have to mean you're discontent with where you live; they simply serve as a source of inspiration. If you start now to discover what delights you, your dream notebook will be a great reference when you are ready to decorate a room.

> Nothing happens unless first a dream.
>
> **Carl Sandburg**

My initial consultation with clients always begins with the same first step. Before I go to their homes, I ask clients to select at least three magazine pictures of rooms they love. This helps focus and expedite decorating by communicating the overall look my clients are trying to achieve.

When doing a weekend retreat with women, I sometimes ask them to bring several home magazines. During a breakout session, we put on some music, sit at round tables, and flip through the magazines. The ladies share magazines and ideas, chatting among themselves about what they like and why. I walk around the room, answer questions, and help women identify some qualities that seem to be their decorating style. We have a ball! The ladies file their findings in a dream notebook and leave for home with a great start toward discovering their decorating style. Why not plan your own dream session with a few friends?

COLLECT YOUR FAVORITE THINGS

Another fun way to dream and inspire your decorating style is to collect colorful memorabilia that appeals to you. I have a decorative basket I call my "favorite things" box. It holds anything I come across that gives my heart a lift and expresses my personal style. My special basket holds a unique collection of favorite trims, fringes, fabrics, paint swatches, wallpaper cuttings, and more. I may not use these actual items in my home, but they help inspire me with my decorating scheme.

No matter where you are in the decorating process for your home, take time to dream by clipping magazine pictures and collecting samples of your favorite things. Poring over the pleasing photographs and boxed treasures may spark the perfect decorating scheme for your home.

Dreaming doesn't cost you a dime.

Simple Tips

Starting a Dream Notebook

- Purchase several home magazines with titles and covers that appeal to you.

- Flip through pages, looking for anything you love at first sight.

- Rip out the pictures you love.

- Identify particular elements you like by circling them with a black marker.

- Sort magazine clippings by room in a notebook or accordion file.

- As patterns emerge in what catches your eye, you will begin to discover your decorating style.

- Continue to add new pictures, editing out old ones that no longer appeal to you. Most of our decorating styles become more refined over time.

- Have a friend leaf through your book and point out what she notices about your decorating style.

Your dream notebook will help you objectively assess your decorating style, without having to spend a lot of money!

Simple Tips

Creating a "Favorite Things" Box

- Find a decorative shoe box, hatbox, or lidded basket that reflects your style.

- Collect favorite items such as pretty fabric swatches and trims, lovely ribbons, a special piece of stationery, an appealing paint chip, a colorful paper napkin, or a sentimental seashell.

- Use the items in the box for inspiration to help you uncover some of your favorite things. Maybe something you tossed in on a whim will spark a color scheme for your home, or a theme for a particular room.

- Go through the box occasionally, weeding out things that no longer appeal to you.

- Hold on only to what you love, love, love.

My "favorite things" box is like a personal treasure chest of beautiful gems collected over time.

Simply Scheming

After you've been up in the clouds dreaming, it's time to come to reality and start planning for your home. Now you are ready to scheme. Scheming is developing an actual plan for decorating your home. Whether you are just beginning to decorate your home or you simply need a fresh look, the starting point is the same.

START WITH WHAT YOU HAVE AND LOVE

Few of us start the decorating process with absolutely nothing. We have all collected things along life's way. Clear off your kitchen or dining room table and go shopping in your own home. Open up your drawers and cabinets. Crawl around your attic. Bring out your prized possessions, the things that hold sentimental value, or items you simply love. Put these treasures on the table and let them spark your decorating scheme.

My brother now has a beautiful emerald green glass candy jar that was once our grandmother's. I know this would be in his cherished collection. Dear friends of ours began their whole decorating scheme around a beautiful Oriental rug passed on to them from relatives and a vibrant oil painting a friend painted for them.

Few of us start the decorating process with absolutely nothing.

What are some of the special items in your home? Your great aunt's mantel clock, a collection of old books, a blue-and-white porcelain urn, a botanical print, or your mother's silver tea service could be just the thing to inspire your decorating.

HAVE A SIGNATURE COLOR

Let a favorite color be your common thread woven room by room throughout your home. Yellow is my signature color. Almost every room of our home has at least a touch of yellow. When playing board games with my nieces and nephews, they always give me the yellow game piece, because they know it's my favorite color. What is your signature color? Does your home have your signature throughout it? When I see certain colors, I think of different friends. Red is Kelly. Raspberry is Brenda. Burgundy is Carmen.

FIND A PALETTE FABRIC

Once you've unveiled your prized possessions and identified your signature color, find a palette fabric. This is my favorite step when helping clients! When an artist begins a painting, he stands before an empty canvas holding a palette that contains all of the colors he will use. Imagine your home as an empty canvas and your palette fabric as the rainbow of colors you want to use in your rooms. Decorate with your palette fabric throughout your central living area wherever you want — on pillows, window treatments, a table skirt, or upholstered furniture. Having a palette fabric is a foolproof formula for decorating your whole home because it provides visual flow between your rooms while still allowing each room to have its own distinctive personality.

A palette fabric is a foolproof formula for decorating your whole home.

Perhaps your palette fabric for the living room is a fresh, floral pattern of vibrant red, yellow, blue, and green on a white background. The blue and yellow might inspire a cheery color scheme for your kitchen. The soothing green could create a lovely look for your bedroom. The rich red could be a dramatic backdrop for your dining room walls. And red, white, and blue could make a fun color scheme for a child's bedroom.

A client friend of mine asked me to help her with her home when she was already midway through the decorating process. While many of her selections were lovely, they were not visually cohesive. As soon as I observed the situation, I knew she simply needed the right palette fabric to get her on track. Searching around, we found a beautiful cotton fabric of green, blue, and golden fruit on a rich cranberry background. We bought a yard, draped it in the main living area, and let the family live with it for a week. Once the palette fabric was unanimously agreed upon, we ordered it from an outlet store. When we covered the armless chairs around her pine kitchen table with the new palette fabric, we had a great starting point for the rest of the home. We painted the entry and living area walls a soft, golden yellow and the dining room walls cranberry red. Immediately, the pieces began to fall into place.

MIX-AND-MATCH FABRICS

With palette fabric in hand, you are ready to begin selecting complementary fabrics for your decorating scheme. A tasteful mixture of fabrics can bring intimacy to any room.

Mixing fabrics can be a fun step in decorating. But remember, "haste makes waste," so make your first trip to the fabric store to simply get inspiration and direction. When you walk in, browse the aisles of beautiful fabrics looking for swatches of fabrics that might enhance the decorating scheme you are working on. Don't think about what fabrics will go where, just gather snips and swatches of anything that appeals.

She selects wool and flax.
Proverbs 31:13

When home, lay all your fabric findings and trims on the floor and admire your treasures. Piece by piece, edit until you come up with the winning combination. Then play "dress up" with the room, pinning the swatches on the furniture and pillows you plan to recover or replace, and draping your windows with a fabric you might consider using for window treatments. Finally, step back and visualize how the fabrics will look in the completed room.

Once you've decided what fabrics will go where, you are ready to buy. If you need yards and yards of a selected fabric, as for upholstery or windows, purchase a "safeguard" yard first. Take it home and look at the large piece to assure you are satisfied. If you still like the fabric, the yard can be used in your room. If not, you prevented a decorating disaster!

PIN UP IDEAS

As you develop your decorating scheme, pin your collection of fabric swatches, paint chips, wallcoverings, and furniture ideas on a bulletin board. Prop the board up in the room you are planning to decorate and edit it as your ideas evolve.

My first job as an interior designer was in hotel and restaurant design with the Marriott Corporation. After assembling presentation boards for proposed decorating schemes, I came to realize what an invaluable tool this is in the planning process. It allows you to visualize a room as a whole before you begin decorating.

CONSIDER FUNCTION

Homes are for living — and life changes. So throw out room labels and think about your lifestyle, your family needs, and how you can best utilize the space you have.

If you have young children, how can your home best accommodate your current needs? Maybe your dining room should become a temporary playroom. Perhaps you have considered working out of your home. Do you have a guest room that can become a home office? Have the kids moved out and now you have an empty nest? Rediscover an old hobby and transform a bedroom into a sewing room or craft room. Does the living room you never use have a beautiful fireplace? Why not bring in your dining room table, add some bookcases, and turn it into a cozy library/dining room?

> Understanding space is the first step towards transforming it.
>
> **Julie Iovine**

In our current home, a small, unused guest room sat adjacent to our modest-sized master bedroom. After much consideration about how to best use the space we have, we decided to knock a hole in the wall and add French doors between the two rooms. It has totally changed our attitude about our bedroom! We cannot wait to call it a day and run to our bedroom "suite." We use the former guest room as a sitting room to curl up and watch a movie or share a meal. Now our bedroom is visually more open and comfortable, and we have also maximized our space to suit our lifestyle.

DECORATE ONE ROOM AT A TIME

To get the greatest impact out of your decorating dollar, focus on one of the rooms where you spend most of your time: your bedroom, bathroom, living area, or kitchen. Completing one room successfully will keep you on track and encourage you to move on to your next project.

If you are building a new home, you will first need to consider the foundational design elements of the whole house — floors, walls, ceilings, lighting, hardware — anything structurally attached to your home. A palette fabric can help you determine room colors, if desired. Once the foundational decisions are made, focus your money and energy on one main room and branch out from there.

Completing one
room successfully
will encourage you!

ESTABLISH A SHOPPING LIST AND BUDGET

Your budget will definitely determine your decorating scheme. If you don't have it, don't spend it! Establish a realistic budget and timetable for your decorating plans. Walk around your room, making a list of everything you want to do from painting the walls to purchasing furniture. Think about any items you want to refinish, reupholster, or replace. Call stores to estimate how much each option will cost. Divide your list into categories of what your budget allows you to do immediately, next year, in two

If you don't have it,
don't spend it!

years. If funds are tight, put your money into the least costly change that will make the most visual impact. For example, consider painting the room now, and later purchasing a quality piece of art to establish a focal point in the room.

Simple Tips

Selecting Your Palette Fabric

- Select one beautiful fabric with appealing colors, pattern, and texture.

- Purchase one yard of the fabric and drape it in your main living area.

- Live with the fabric for a week or so to assure you and your family unanimously agree on it.

- Use this fabric in your main living area wherever you wish, on window treatments, pillows, table skirt, or upholstery.

- If you have a palette fabric with a printed pattern on it, use the colored dots along the selvage edge of the fabric as the formula for selecting each room's unique color scheme.

- Let your palette fabric inspire the color schemes for other rooms throughout your home.

A palette fabric can be a great starting point for decorating or it can pull together what you already have.

simple Tips

Mixing Fabrics

- Color intensity is the key to successful mixing. When mixing fabrics, mix all vibrant, all pastel, or all neutral colors.

- Begin with one large-scale pattern (two large-scale patterns will distract the eyes).

- Add one medium-sized pattern (like a stripe or large check).

- Add small patterns (dots, plaids, stripes, checks, miniprints).

- Anchor the room with at least one solid color.

- For a subtle and sophisticated look, mix textures of solid, neutral fabrics.

- If you need inspiration, refer to your dream notebook and see how the fabrics are combined in rooms you admire.

- You can take the guesswork out of mixing fabrics by relying on manufacturer-selected pattern mixes in fabric and wallpaper books.

The more fabrics and patterns you mix, and the bolder the colors, the livelier the look!

Forming the Framework

The earth was formless and empty.
—Genesis 1:2

2

*I*n the beginning, the earth was formless and empty — a blank canvas. Then God, the Artist of the universe, began creating his world in a deliberate and orderly fashion. The very first thing he did was form the framework, painting the sky, land, and sea.

You can use the same masterful plan in decorating your own little world. When possible, before you put a single piece of furniture in your room, prepare the framework. Take time to get the "bones" of your room right, selecting the appropriate floor, wall, and ceiling finishes.

Forming the framework first will provide you with the perfect backdrop for the next step of decorating, filling your home with furniture and accessories. Make the bones of your room beautiful, and anything will look good in it, no matter how modest. It's like getting your body into shape. If you have taken the time to care for your physical frame, a simple black dress looks and feels great when you put it on.

When making flooring and wall treatment selections, you can choose to have your floors and walls be a subtle backdrop for your furnishings, or have them make a striking statement. Remember, you are the artist, and your home is your canvas!

> . . . the skies proclaim the
> work of his hands.
>
> **Psalm 19:1**

Simply Floors

The first step to consider when forming the framework for your home is your floors. Floors form the foundation of any home. Flooring selections will be some of the most important and costly decorating decisions you make.

More than likely, your primary flooring surfaces have already been determined, and decorative rugs are all you need to add. If, however, you are building or renovating, selecting the appropriate flooring can lay the proper groundwork for a beautiful home. Once you have a solid foundation, your other selections will fall into place with ease and grace.

There are several factors to consider when selecting floors:

- What is the room's function? Will you be eating there?

- Consider your lifestyle. Do you have active children or pets?

- Think about traffic patterns. Is the room in a major thoroughfare of the home?

- Is the flooring easy to maintain? How often are you willing to clean it?

- How long do you anticipate living in your home? How long will the floor last?

- What is your budget? Should you splurge on your floors now and hold off on other things that can be more easily added later?

- Consider the architecture of your home. A southwestern home might lend itself to a terra-cotta tile, while a traditional home may call for the warmth and charm of hardwood floors.

- What selection is most suitable for the climate where you live? A home by the beach beckons for the cool surface of ceramic tile.

- How will the floor surfaces flow? Too many surface changes can make a space seem chopped up and small. Yet, two different flooring materials and textures can add interest. If your surfaces change from room to room, unify the flooring with a similar color.

- What look do you want? Casual, elegant, rustic, or contemporary?

When selecting your flooring surfaces, there are choices galore, from hardwood to tile, carpet to vinyl. Visit several stores before making any major decisions. Different places will offer a variety of options and pricing. As you shop, you will notice flooring falls into two general categories: hard surfaces and soft surfaces.

> A good floor says that the entire foundation of the room is sound.
>
> **Mark Hampton**

Hard surfaces are natural materials like wood, tile, and stone. Because God created these materials, they cannot be surpassed for beauty. Each brings life and a touch of outdoors into a room. Soft surfaces include floor coverings such as carpet, rugs, and vinyl. Though hard surfaces are generally more costly than soft surfaces, their durability and low maintenance must be factored into their price. If ever there is a time and place to indulge, consider your floors. When possible, use natural materials to give your home integrity and lasting beauty.

Naturally Beautiful Floors

I love the simple beauty of wood floors. They are casual, practical, and unpretentious, and will work just about anywhere in your home (with the exception of the bathroom, where they can warp). We have installed the wood floors in our home in stages. When we first bought our house and the rooms were empty, we installed white oak hardwoods in some of the downstairs rooms. Recently, we came back and completed the job, installing wood floors in our living room and dining room. Though it would have been much easier to install it all at once, it would have overextended us financially — and no amount of beauty is worth financial stress.

Despite the temporary inconvenience of sanding, dust, noise, and mess, our wood floors were worth the wait. With their medium fruitwood stain, they never look dirty, and blend with any furniture finish. And even better than their natural beauty, they are a breeze to clean with a damp mop.

There are many other beautiful natural materials that can transform the ambience of your room to whatever look you want, from casual to elegant. Stone floors can be anything from rough slate slabs to limestone to polished marble squares. Tiles can range from earthy terra-cotta to bright ceramic to hand-painted glazed.

Consider natural materials in places with high traffic and visibility. A client of mine loves to entertain. When helping select flooring for their front foyer and kitchen, we chose large, octagonal terra-cotta tiles. The tiles' warm, natural look created a beautiful and lasting foundation for some of the major traffic areas in their home.

> Because God created natural materials, they cannot be surpassed for beauty.

THE VALUE OF VINYL

Soft surfaces can also prove to be an attractive foundation for a room. Popular for kitchens and bathrooms, vinyl flooring is a cost-effective choice for durability and low maintenance. Vinyl flooring is available in sheets or tiles. Vinyl sheets allow for installation without seams; however, if the vinyl is damaged in any area, the whole floor requires replacing. Vinyl tiles allow for easy replacement of damaged tiles and more custom pattern designs, but dirt can collect in the seams. Both types of vinyl flooring are available in many different qualities and prices. If you choose to use vinyl flooring, I recommend keeping the design as simple as possible and not attempting to duplicate marble or other natural materials. It tends to accentuate their artificiality.

In our first home, our kitchen floors were a clean, white sheet vinyl . . . that is, for about one day! After spending far too much time on my hands and knees cleaning those floors, I wised up and purchased large, natural, sisal rugs to cover much of the floor space. It proved an inexpensive solution to keeping our floors clean and attractive. When your floors look clean, your house feels clean — and that feels good!

When your floors look clean, your house feels clean — and that feels good!

ROLL OUT THE RUGS

Rugs are a great soft surface that can enhance your floors. They are available in an endless selection of patterns, textures, colors, and prices to suit any style and budget. Rugs can protect your floors, define a space, and unify furnishings. They add warmth, character, and comfort.

I love to scatter cotton rag rugs anywhere that needs a splash of color and a touch of texture. I use them often in my own home and for clients in front of a kitchen sink, in bathrooms, beside a bed, or in front of an entry door. They are reasonably priced, available in a rainbow of colors, and reversible.

Some of my favorite rugs are sisal, jute, or seagrass. Each is natural and woven from plant fibers. These types of rugs are extremely durable, reasonably priced, and available in many home stores and catalogs. They can be somewhat rough on the feet, so I use them primarily in areas where people won't be sitting on the floor. Rugs made of natural materials can be used anywhere, from the most elegant home to a casual seaside cottage. They can also be installed wall-to-wall as carpeting. Seagrass with latex backing is my preferred choice, and I use it often for clients. For a custom look, hand-paint a design on a natural woven rug.

Another advantage of rugs is their ability to change the look and feel of a room instantly. When the crisp chill of fall comes, I roll out weathered Oriental rugs passed on to us from family. They lend an immediate sense of coziness and character to our wood floors. When spring is in the air, I fold up those treasured rugs and let the beauty of the wood floors stand on its own. In other areas, I put out natural seagrass rugs (with latex backing) for a bit of texture and casualness. Change helps keep any home fresh and alive.

COMFORT WITH CARPET

Wall-to-wall carpeting is another soft surface for floors. Carpet brings color, texture, and warmth to a room for a moderate cost. The choices are vast, and it is well worth educating yourself on the differences before you make a selection.

Change helps keep any home fresh and alive.

When purchasing carpet, think quality first and then color. The denser (thicker) the carpet, the more comfortable, quieter, longer lasting, and costly it will be. To test for durability, bend the carpet back on itself. If you can see the backing easily, it is loosely woven and less durable.

For unity, I recommend one type of carpet be installed throughout the home. I prefer a neutral, tightly woven carpet that will provide a subtle backdrop for furnishings.

Whether covering your floors with rugs or carpeting, proper padding is critical. It provides support and comfort, absorbs sound and foot traffic, prevents slipping, and enhances the life of the carpet or rug. It's wise to purchase the best padding you can afford.

Remember, floors are the foundation of your rooms. Once you have made the best possible selection for your floors, given your budget, you are already well on your way to creating a beautiful home.

Simple Tips
Selecting Wood Floors

- Use a medium fruitwood stain to create a warm, neutral background that conceals dirt and blends beautifully with any wood furniture.

- Use a satin polyurethane finish for subtle luster. A matte finish can appear dull, while a gloss finish can appear artificial.

- Oak is the most popular hardwood floor. It is less susceptible to scratches and dents than pine. Available in red or white oak, white oak has a finer, more subtle wood grain than red.

- Pine is the most popular softwood floor. With little grain variation and much distressing, it gives a casual feel.

- Consider painting or bleaching a wood floor for a custom casual look.

- If you have stairs, leave them bare of carpet and stain or paint them. Though a bit noisier, they will be easier to keep clean.

I love the simple beauty of wood floors!

Simple Tips

Selecting Tile, Marble, or Stone

- To hide dirt, use natural materials with color and texture variances.

- Consider light-colored materials to make a room seem larger.

- Lay tile on diagonal to visually expand a room.

- For an elegant look, use marble.

- For a rustic, relaxed feeling, use brick, textured tiles, and stones.

- Use large stone or 12" x 12" or 16" x 16" tile to save money and visually expand a space.

- Ceramic tile is available in a variety of colors and patterns and is the most frequently used material for bathrooms.

- Terra-cotta tiles give a natural, earthy look.

- For a custom look, use hand-painted, glazed tiles.

- The harder the floor material, the more strain on your feet, legs, and back, and the more easily fragile items shatter. To soften and warm the touch, use rugs in areas where you will be frequently standing.

- For a subtle look, use grout tinted to match material. For a dramatic look, use contrasting grout.

Light-colored 12" x 12" ceramic floor tiles visually expand the tiny master bathroom.

Simple Tips
Selecting Carpet

- Install tightly woven, stain resistant carpet in high traffic areas.

- To hide footprints, use a loop pile, berber carpet.

- Nylon carpet is the most commonly used and is available in a wide range of colors. It is the strongest man-made fiber and easy to clean.

- Olefin carpet is the fastest growing fiber today. It is used for loop carpeting and available in neutral shades. Olefin carpet is great for high traffic areas, but has a harder feel.

- Wool carpet is the most deluxe and expensive. Its natural fiber makes it soft, extremely durable, and easy to clean.

- Use a dark, patterned carpet to make your space cozy.

- Use a light, solid carpet to visually enlarge your space.

- Before purchasing, view a large sample in your home to assure the carpet is the desired color.

- Walk on your carpet choice with your bare feet to assure its comfort.

- To avoid excess seams, select a carpet that is as wide or wider than your room. Most carpets are 12 feet wide, but some are available up to 18 feet wide.

- Have carpet installed by an experienced, licensed, and bonded professional to avoid unsightly seams and improperly stretched carpet.

When selecting carpet, think quality first, then color.

Simple Tips
Selecting Rugs

- Use a rug on top of a carpet to define a conversation area.

- Area rugs are commonly available in 4 x 6, 5 x 7, 6 x 9, 8 x 10, 9 x 12, 12 x 15, and 16 x 20 feet.

- Determine the size rug you need by the placement of your furniture.

- Keep upholstered furniture either all on or off your rug to keep furniture legs balanced.

- For your dining room, make sure that the rug is large enough so all chairs will remain on the rug when they're pulled out from the table. If the table expands with leaves, make sure the rug accommodates the full span of table and chairs.

- Oriental rugs are durable rugs made in rich colors. Their beautiful patterns are often named after their place of origin. Oriental rugs are moderately priced if they are new and manufactured, but can be expensive treasures if old and hand-knotted.

- For a casual country look, try a braided rug. Braided rugs are made of strips of cloth braided and stitched together.

- Hooked rugs have a thick pile made of yarn pulled through a backing. Most have charming, colorful patterns.

- Dhurrie and kilims are flat, wool, or cotton rugs in various patterns, woven in India. Dhurries have muted colors, while kilims have rich colors.

Varying the patterns and textures of rugs adds interest to the front foyer and beyond.

Simply Walls

Walls form the framework of any room. They cover more space than any other single element. Therefore, what you choose to do with your walls greatly impacts the overall atmosphere of your home.

OPEN UP

Before selecting your wall treatments, think about the walls themselves. Does the placement of your walls suit your lifestyle and likings? Many homes today have open floor plans that suit our busy and casual living. If, however, you reside in a home where there are lots of walls, think about what minor changes could enhance your floor plan. If possible, make the needed changes as you form the framework of your room. Now is the time to consider knocking down a wall, opening up a room, widening an opening, adding French doors, or removing unneeded doors. Simple structural changes like these can totally change the feel and flow of your rooms, without being a major expense. Before you begin, have a professional builder look at your wall structure to determine what is involved. If the wall you wish to remove is load-bearing, you will need to add additional support to keep your home structurally sound.

When we moved into our current home, we began by assessing the flow of our rooms. The rooms off the foyer were not very visible, and the initial impression upon entering the house was confining. We first widened the opening from the foyer into the living room by a foot, to make it more accessible and inviting. Then we created a six-foot opening to add French doors between the living room and family room. Now when you walk into our front foyer it feels much more open, and your eyes can see into the rooms beyond. These two small structural changes totally transformed our living areas and our use and enjoyment of our home.

WHAT TO DO WITH YOUR WALLS?

If you have your walls where you want them to be, how will you treat them to enhance your room? There are many decorative choices for walls, from paint to wallcovering, wood trim or paneling, fabric, mirrors, or murals.

To determine the most suitable wall treatment for a room, consider the following needs and decorating style preferences:

- What are the functions of the room?

- Is the room in a high traffic area? If the walls will need to be cleaned often, you will want to consider satin or gloss paint, vinyl-coated wallcovering, or wood paneling.

- What mood do you wish to create? Do you want to create a cozy or an open feeling?

> Picking that perfect paint color is the cherry on the sundae, the final, finishing touch for your walls.

- Do you like to make artwork the focal point of your room? If so, consider a simple backdrop.

- Do you want a lively look? If so, consider a vibrant wallcovering.

- Do you like to have flexibility in your decorating? Painting your walls may be the answer.

- What is your budget? Do you plan to treat the walls yourself or hire a professional?

POPULAR PAINT

Paint is the most popular and practical wall treatment. In most cases, it is my preferred option for decorating walls simply. Paint is the easiest, quickest, and most economical way to transform a room. If you are on a limited budget, yet want to make a noticeable improvement to a room, pull out the paintbrush.

When selecting paint colors for several rooms in your home at one time, look to your palette fabric for guidance. The colored dots along the selvage of your fabric can act as your rainbow of paint choices for rooms. If you are planning on using wallcovering in some rooms, make those selections before your paint colors. It is far easier to select a paint color to match a wallcovering than to find a wallcovering that works with a paint color. Picking that perfect paint color is the cherry on the sundae, the final, finishing touch for your walls.

When it comes to selecting a specific paint color, there are several ways to simplify the process. Any fabric or surface color can be computer-matched into a paint. I use this method to mix a paint to go with a particular fabric, or to match one manufacturer's color to another company's paint. If you see a paint in an existing home that you like, inquire what it is. Keep in mind that the light levels of different rooms will affect the look of the color. You can also choose a preselected color from a designer paint collection. These collections narrow down your choices, helping take some of the guesswork out of picking paint. Lastly, if you have a friend who has an eye for color, let her help you make a selection.

Though I've picked out hundreds of paint colors over the years, I still never assume a color that looks perfect on a paint chip will look the same on the wall. Test a quart of your selected paint before you purchase gallons for the job. It costs the same amount for the wrong color as it does for the perfect color!

Though I personally prefer the simple look of plain, painted walls in yummy colors, there are many interesting decorative faux or "false" finishes that can take your walls from boring to beautiful. Treatments such as sponging, rag rolling, combing, glazing, marbleizing, stenciling, and trompe l'oeil (fool the eye) all give the illusion of texture and depth. To achieve these looks, you can hire a professional, or take a class or watch a video to learn them. Many faux finishes are not difficult to paint, but it's a good idea to practice on a sample piece of foamboard before tackling a whole room.

Marvelous Murals

Painted murals can also make unique and beautiful backdrops for rooms. Why not paint a mural in your nursery or child's room to create a fun and colorful setting? Use an overhead projector to transfer designs you want to paint onto the walls. For a young boy's bedroom, try a forest of trees painted on the walls and turn his bunk bed into an adventurous tree house. For a girl's room, cover the walls with a colorful garden of hand-painted flowers and place window boxes beneath the interior windows. Or paint or install a white picket fence along a wall, with a soft blue sky behind it. Build a simple headboard for the bed in the shape of a house, with shelves to hold her favorite treasures. For a simple, sophisticated touch, paint an inspiring quote or Scripture on a wall.

Let your imagination soar, and your walls carry out your fantasy. All it takes is some inexpensive paint and the courage to try. If you tire of or outgrow the look, a few coats of fresh paint will cover it up!

Wonderful Wallcoverings

Wallcoverings are another easy way to cover your walls and give instant atmosphere. Just walk into a wallpaper store, and you will see there are choices galore, from lively patterns to soothing stripes to subtle textures. Each gives a totally different look to your room.

Wallcoverings add life to forgotten areas like stairwells, hallways, or foyers. They distract the eye from damaged, uneven, or awkward walls. And, when available, coordinating borders and fabrics can make developing your decorating scheme simple.

A wonderful wallcovering in a front foyer can be a welcome introduction to the colors in your home. Clients of mine purchased a beautiful old home overlooking the rolling hills of Virginia horse country. We settled on covering the walls of their sun-filled foyer with a free-flowing floral pattern in soothing pastels on a soft vanilla background. With its open pattern, the warm and friendly wallcovering welcomes guests into the foyer and invites them up the stairway. This delightful wallcovering provided a colorful palette for selecting paints in the adjacent rooms and served as the unifying component for their decorating scheme.

I particularly like striped wallcoverings. They are crisp, clean, and simple and provide a colored, patterned background without competing with artwork or a room's furnishings. Though most walls in our home are painted, two of our three bathrooms are covered in cheerful stripes. I never tire of their look.

WHAT ABOUT WOOD?

Wood paneling or trim enhances walls by giving them dimension. Simple wood touches such as a decorative chair rail, wainscoting (wood material that covers the lower portion of a wall), or a beautiful crown molding are classic architectural details that make a difference.

If your dark paneling has a poor quality veneer and is zapping energy from your room, consider deglossing, priming, and then painting it. In doing so, you will bring light and charm into the room without losing the lovely wood details. I adore the cottage look of painted paneling and use this treatment often. In areas that need to be especially durable, install tongue-and-groove paneling and then paint it. A treatment often used in commercial restaurants, I also love to use this finish in kitchens, bathrooms, bedrooms — anywhere that needs subtle interest that will wear like iron.

FABRIC WALLS

Fabric can be used on walls for a touch of warmth, texture, and variation. A client in Texas had a paneled living room that needed some interest. We opened one of the walls to the adjacent family room, so the fireplace could be in view, then pickled the wood wainscoting, trim, and bookcases to slightly lighten the room. For the finishing touch, we installed fabric above the wainscoting. To do this, we first put quilting batting onto the entire wall surface to add thickness, stapling the batting along the edges of the walls. Then we stitched the selvages together of several widths of a plaid wool fabric. Holding the fabric on top of the batting, we stapled along the edges of the walls and cut around the openings and windows. Lastly, we covered the staples by gluing a decorative cording along the edges of the walls. With its new fabric walls and open look, the room now radiates life and warmth.

While shirred fabric on rods makes for a lovely, cozy look, it can, however, take a large amount of fabric. Because of this, it may be most suitable for use in small rooms, like powder rooms.

THE MAGIC OF MIRRORS

A wall-to-wall mirror can lighten and brighten a room and visually double the space. If you have a small bathroom, consider mirroring from the countertop to the ceiling in front of the sink, and on both sides too, if there are walls. This simple wall treatment will open up your bathroom immensely. If desired, decorative wood trim can be used to frame out the mirrors. When installing wide spans of mirror, use beveled mirror strips to give a finished look and conceal seams.

Before covering a whole wall with mirror, consider the view that will be reflected. Is it attractive enough to duplicate, or would it reflect something unsightly like the back of a toilet or unfinished wood? When helping clients in Florida decorate their waterfront condominium, we decided to mirror an entire side wall of their main living area. The mirror not only visually expanded the room, but reflected the incredible view of beautiful blue water and passing boats.

NATURALLY BEAUTIFUL STONE, BRICK, AND TILE

For a splurge, consider using a natural material such as stone, brick, or tile to give texture, beauty, and warmth to accent a wall. Natural materials are easy to maintain, extremely durable, and lend a sense of stability and permanence to a home. I love to use stack stone or old brick for fireplace walls.

A friend in Atlanta has custom tiles on the kitchen wall behind her stovetop. The tiles are each hand-painted with one of the fruit of the Spirit: love, joy, peace, patience, kindness, goodness, faithfulness, gentleness, and self-control. What a perfect place to display such an important reminder!

THE FORGOTTEN FIFTH WALL

While preparing your walls, don't overlook your ceiling. Ceilings cover the same amount of space as floors, yet are seldom considered when decorating. In neglecting the ceiling as part of the whole background, we miss a great opportunity to enhance the ambience of the room. From borders to beams to trim to skylights to simply painting an interesting color, the sky is the limit when it comes to ceiling options!

To lend an intimate feeling to a dining room or powder room, consider painting the ceiling to match the walls. When decorating a powder room wallpapered in a green and white stripe, we painted the ceiling the

> In decorating, one thing always leads to another.
>
> **Alexandra Stoddard**

same green as the stripe. With white crown molding, the green ceiling gave the perfect finishing touch.

LET IT FLOW

Whatever you choose from the vast array of wall treatments, keep in mind the visual flow of the walls from room to room. The best way to do this is to lay samples of paint colors and wallcovering selections side by side in the order of your floor plan. Though each room has its own personality, the overall visual flow of your home looks best when rooms transition smoothly. Having a palette fabric or palette wallcovering in your main living area will help with this transition. Walls of the same color or similar shade (i.e., soft yellow/soft green) create a spacious feeling and draw the eye into adjoining rooms. Rooms that vary significantly in wall color (i.e., a cobalt room adjoining a white room) create interest and establish distinctively different spaces.

Simple Tips

Selecting a Paint

- Proper preparation of wall surface is critical for an attractive paint job.

- Once you have selected your paint color, purchase only one quart of the paint.

- Apply two coats of paint on a large piece of foamboard (available in arts and craft stores) or Sheetrock.

- To confirm the color, prop your board in the room you plan to paint and observe it in the daytime and nighttime.

- A paint color appears darker on walls than on a paint chip. A good rule of thumb is to purchase a paint one shade lighter on the paint chart than what you think you want.

- A paint color looks darker in a room with few or no windows.

- Light paint colors make a room seem larger; dark paint colors make a room cozy and intimate.

- Latex paint will not adhere on top of existing oil paint.

- Latex paint with a flat finish has a matte, somewhat chalky look and is the best finish to conceal flawed walls.

- Latex satin or eggshell finishes have a slight sheen, hide fingerprints, and are excellent for high traffic areas.

- Oil-base semigloss and high gloss finishes are excellent for trim, woodwork, doors, cabinets.

- The higher the gloss, the easier the paint will be to clean, the lighter the color will look, and the more surface defects will show due to shine.

*Paint is the easiest, quickest, most
economical way to transform a room.*

Simple Tips

Selecting a Wallcovering

- Before going to the wallpaper store, decide what look you want in the room. Are you looking for something subtle, dramatic, a texture, stripes, floral, mini-print?

- Make note of what you're looking for to avoid getting distracted.

- Take your fabric or some color reference to the store.

- Quickly flip through top right corners of pages to see the color palette of inks. Each book has a range of ink colors used for all their patterns.

- Once you find a book that has the colors you're looking for, leaf through the pages quickly to see if anything catches your eye, marking any pages that interest you.

- Take home any book that has an excellent possibility.

- Prop up the books in the room where you plan to use the wallcovering and study them in the daytime and nighttime.

- Once you've made your choice, get the largest sample possible (buy a roll if necessary). Tack it to your wall and live with it for a few days to assure you like the look.

- Before hanging, check to assure all rolls are the same dye lot or run number.

- For easy removal in the future, coat walls with wallcovering primer before hanging your paper.

- A large patterned wallcovering makes a small room appear larger.

- Embossed wallcoverings add texture and can be painted a color of your choice.

*The striped wallcovering in the powder room
provides a simple backdrop for accessories.*

Simple Tips

Selecting Wood Wall Treatments

- To break up walls and give visual variety, add a chair rail and wainscoting (wood detail) on the bottom half of the wall.

- Add a small, flat piece of molding several inches below your crown molding. Paint both moldings and wall space between moldings the same trim color to give the illusion of one large piece.

- Add paneling to a room that lacks dimension or architectural interest.

- Wood paneling provides extra insulation and sound control.

- Wood paneling is a durable solution for high traffic areas and to cover damaged walls.

- Sheet paneling (4' x 8' sheets of plywood with wood veneer) is the least expensive type of wood paneling.

- Tongue-and-groove planks provide dimension and quality, and are available in pine, poplar, and cedar.

- Custom woodwork gives the most flexibility in wood wall treatments, allowing you to select the wood, plank style, and millwork detailing—but is also the costliest.

- Stained paneling lends warmth and natural beauty to a room.

- Painted paneling gives a charming cottage look.

- To paint existing paneling, wipe with a deglosser, prime, then paint.

Painted wood paneling lends a touch of charm to our master bedroom sitting area.

Simple Tips
Selecting Ceiling Treatments

- Let your ceiling slightly reflect your walls by adding one cup of your wall color to each gallon of white ceiling paint.

- For an airy look, paint a ceiling sky blue. Then, use white spray paint to create light mists of cloud, and accent by sponging with white paint.

- To visually lower a high ceiling, paint it a tone darker than the walls.

- Purchase glow-in-the-dark paint and paint stars on a child's bedroom ceiling.

- For a subtle decorative touch, use embossed wallcovering on a ceiling and paint it, if desired.

- For a touch of class, surround a chandelier ceiling cap with a round decorative medallion and paint it to match your room trim.

- Add beams or tongue-and-groove panels to high ceilings for architectural interest.

- For a cozy, intimate feel, cover the ceiling in a small room with shirred fabric.

- Add a skylight to any ceiling whose room lacks sufficient window light.

- Install a ceiling fan to circulate room air, as well as give a casual decorative look.

- For drama and to visually enlarge a room, expand your ceiling up to the roofline.

- For an outdoor awning feel, cover an angled ceiling with stripe wallpaper or fabric.

Painting the ceiling to match the green stripes in the wallcovering gives instant intimacy to the powder room.

Filling Your Home

Once God formed the world, he filled it with life.

3

*A*fter God *formed* the world by creating the land, sea, and sky, he *filled* it with life — plants and trees, fish and birds, animals and man. Likewise, once you have formed the framework for your home — the floors and walls and ceilings — it's time to fill your world with the things that bring it life — furniture, window treatments, and accessories.

When God filled the earth, he added each element in a logical order. He first made the plants and seed-bearing trees to provide food. Then, he created the living animals and man that would need to be nourished from the vegetation. Similarly, there is a logical order for filling your home. First, you should acquire furniture to serve your most primary needs of sleeping and eating. Then you can focus on the additional furniture, window treatments, and accessories that bring comfort, function, and beauty into your home.

Though your decorating purchases may be determined by your budget, when possible, focus on the large items first and gradually fill in with smaller pieces. The steps that follow will provide a logical order for prioritizing your purchasing decisions.

Simply Furniture

Just as the floors, walls, and ceilings form the framework for your home, your furniture begins to fill it. Each piece of furniture serves as a basic building block for beautiful living. If your budget is limited, like most, be grateful. Houses that are filled all at once with a truck-load of furniture lack heart and a sense of history. The most beautiful homes are furnished one piece at a time. Whatever your budget, take your time as you acquire your furniture. When you go slowly, you go wisely. The furniture selections you make are significant, and if you make quality purchases, they will last a lifetime.

> I prefer furniture that appears to have been collected, piece by piece, over many years.
>
> **Mario Buatta**

YOUR FURNITURE FAMILY

View your furniture pieces like members of a family. Each person has a unique and individual personality. Each has his own story behind who he is and when he came into the family. And the addition of each family member brings more life and energy to the whole. If you are just beginning to decorate your home, focus on acquiring a few basic, beautiful pieces and anticipate, in time, adding new members to your furniture family.

> When you go slowly, you go wisely.

75

THE BASIC BUILDING BLOCKS

There are three major furniture purchases you will need to make at some point to create a comfortable, functional, and beautiful home. Each helps to meet a primary need:

- A comfortable bed to give you the proper rest and necessary sleep
- A table and chairs for meals to nourish and strengthen your body
- A satisfying sofa to relax and enjoy relationships

Once this primary furniture is in place, add other pieces one by one. Dressers, chests, side tables, coffee tables, armoires, chairs, and ottomans will enhance your living all the more.

SUITABLE STYLE

If you have collected magazine clippings into a dream notebook or accordion file, then you already have a reference for your decorating style and the furniture that appeals to you. Before making any major purchasing decisions, consider several factors:

- Does this furniture reflect my decorating style?
- Does its beauty stand on its own?
- Is it functional?
- Is it comfortable?
- Is it well-constructed?

> Each piece of furniture should have a story to tell.
>
> **Alexandra Stoddard**

> If you wisely invest in beauty, it will remain with you all the days of your life.
>
> **Frank Lloyd Wright**

Try to create a balance between the furniture's look and livability. Find furniture that is pleasing to your eye, yet suitable for your needs. If you go for classic lines, good proportion, and quality construction, your furniture will stand the test of time.

A Fabulous Focal Point

Every room in a home needs a focal point—a starting point for the eye to jump to and the furniture to surround. A focal point can be an architectural element like a fireplace, a bay window, or a built-in bookshelf. Or you can also create a focal point with a piece of furniture, such as a bed, china cabinet, armoire, or even artwork.

Let your favorite pieces become a focal point. When helping a client to make her front foyer warm and welcoming, I didn't have to go far to find the focus we needed. Hidden in a dark corner of her living room, I discovered a beautiful mahogany secretary, originally her grandmother's. We brought it into the foyer and put it center stage on the wall facing the front door, filling it with books, plants, and adding a charming side chair. The foyer came alive, and the beautiful piece could be enjoyed by all who entered.

THE ART OF ARRANGING

Many people think they need bigger homes when often all they need to do is make better use of the space they have. To get the best use out of every square foot of your home, assure each room is multifunctional. Your dining room can do double duty as a library, office, or eating area. Your living room can be a game room, media room, casual dining room, or reading room.

Easy conversation, accessible traffic flow, and flexible activities are all qualities to keep in mind as you select and arrange your furniture. If you buy furniture in classic styles, shapes, and scale, the pieces will look beautiful in different settings and give you flexibility for arranging. Buy a piece because you love it and can use it several places in your home, not because it's the only thing you could find to fit a quirky corner.

Aim for visual balance when arranging furniture in a room. Strive for a mixture of soft, upholstered furniture and hard, wood furniture. Balance the number of exposed wood legs and soft, skirted items in the room.

The living room is often the most challenging room to arrange. As you think about how to place your furniture, consider the following questions:

- What is the focal point?
- How many people do you need to seat?
- What type of seating do you prefer?

- Do you need flexible seating for guests?
- What other activities will take place here?

When rearranging a room, clear out all of the furniture except the sofa. To create the most intimate furniture arrangements, create a conversational area no bigger than 12' x 12' or 14' x 14'. Draw furniture in a few feet from the walls. For interest, try placing your sofa diagonally. A console table or chest behind your sofa will make a great surface for accessories that add light and coziness to your seating.

If you have a large room, create two conversation areas, or have one large seating area and one small seating area composed of two chairs and a table or a single chair and ottoman. Nothing is more inviting than being able to steal away to a secluded corner and curl up in a comfortable chair with a good book!

When arranging a client's living room furniture, I flanked the fireplace with two sofas and placed a large coffee table in the center. But even though drawing the furniture in created a more intimate feeling in the large room, it left a stark, open corner. We then filled the corner with a pub table and four chairs, to be used for meals and games. The arrangement provided both flexibility and function for their busy family.

Another important element of furniture arranging is making sure the furniture will fit comfortably in your room. To accurately visualize the size of each piece, use a measuring tape or place brown mailing paper cut the length and width of your furniture in its future location. Be sure there is adequate accessibility. Also measure doorways, openings, and hallways to be certain new furniture will pass through. Better to be safe than sorry.

Recently, I was about to purchase two club chairs for a living room with limited space. The chairs were to have swivel bases to allow them to be part of the conversation area or turn to watch the television. We had already selected the chair style and fabric when we measured the room and discovered that while the chairs fit in the space where they would be used, there was not adequate room for them to swivel without blocking the traffic flow. Careful measuring prevented an expensive mistake!

BEAUTIFUL BEDS

You spend approximately one-third of your life in your bed. This makes your bed the most used piece of furniture in your home and therefore the most important for your well-being.

> No room will look its best until it is comfortably arranged.
>
> **Mark Hampton**

> One's bedroom should be more than comfortable, it should be intimate.
>
> **Elsie de Wolfe**

A quality mattress and box spring are critical to creating a comfortable bed and providing a good night's sleep. When you're purchasing furniture for sleeping, a comfortable mattress and box spring should come before a beautiful bed frame. If finances are limited, buy the best mattress and box spring possible and place them on a simple metal frame on casters. The first major furniture purchase Bill and I made when we married was a deluxe, extrafirm mattress and box spring set. Though not as beautiful as a high, four-poster bed, we knew the importance of first getting the right foundation for rest.

Once you have the proper foundation laid with your mattress and box spring, a beautiful headboard and footboard can bring personality into your private room. Take the time to dream about what style bed suits you. A rustic iron bed, a casual pine bed, an antique brass bed, a mahogany poster bed, a romantic canopy bed? When you're ready, treat yourself to a beautiful, quality bed frame that you will enjoy for years.

A PLEASING PLACE TO EAT

After a bed, your next major furniture decision will be to buy an attractive and comfortable table and chairs. Together the table and chairs will provide a pleasant place for eating your meals and visiting with family and friends. It's likely you spend more time in your kitchen than in your dining room, so your kitchen table and chairs should take priority over dining room furnishings.

Have fun looking at what shapes, sizes, and styles are available and pleasing to you. Dining tables come round, rectangular, oval, and square. Materials can vary from softwoods such as pine to hardwood such as maple, which can be stained, varnished, or painted. Tables can also be tile-topped or glass-topped, and can have wood, plaster, or iron bases. When you do select a table, make sure it fits your room, allowing at least 36 inches from the table's edge to the wall for adequate traffic flow.

Pine farm tables are a favorite for casual dining and living. Pine gains character with time and wear. The more bangs and nicks the better. If your table serves as a multipurpose surface for sticky fingers, art projects, homework, gift wrapping, letter writing, and more, a pine table might suit your lifestyle beautifully.

If you have a lovely dining room table and chairs, then by all means use them! Don't save the furniture for guests only. Clients of mine eat Sunday suppers in their dining room almost every week. Though the meals are casual, they can enjoy their beautiful furniture and use it as special time to teach their children about manners and etiquette.

A Satisfying Sofa

A quality, comfortable sofa is the largest, most important upholstered piece for your home. A sofa anchors a room, all other furnishings revolving around it. It brings color, comfort, and coziness to a living area. It can set the whole tone for comfort in your room, affecting how often, you, your family, and friends sit down and relax.

In most cases, you get what you pay for when it comes to a sofa. A quality-constructed sofa with classic lines can last years and simply be reupholstered or slipcovered for a fresh look. Slipcovering is less costly than reupholstering and works best with lightweight fabrics such as cotton, linen, or denim. I enjoy the casual, comfortable look of slipcovers. If you have young children, slipcovers in durable, washable fabrics are a great option.

For versatility in decorating, cover your sofa and other large upholstery items in solid, durable fabric. Incorporate busy patterns on less expensive items that can be changed more easily, like pillows and window treatments.

While working with one client, I covered two large sofas and two club chairs all in off-white, stain-resistant muslin. The furniture sat on top of a beautiful Oriental rug that provided the color palette for the room. For a splash of color on the sofas, we added big, down pillows in plaid fabric with blue brush fringe. The neutral upholstery created a subtle and flexible backdrop for the colorful accessories.

WHAT NEXT?

Once you've gotten the basics in place — your bed, dining table and chairs, and sofa — fill in your rooms with less costly pieces that can be easily moved between rooms. Enjoy the journey of collecting favorite pieces over time, keeping in mind that comfort, materials, and construction are as important as style.

COMFORTING CHAIRS

Cozy chairs encourage relaxation. Do you have a favorite chair you can steal away to? What style chair suits your personality? Do you prefer a casual, overstuffed club chair, a sleek, stretching leather recliner, or a rustic, wooden rocker? When you purchase chairs for your home, try to purchase them in pairs, and if they are skirted, add swivel bases. As pairs, you can display them together or in separate rooms, and the swivel base helps to create a comfortable conversation area.

If there's a man in your home, does he have a comfortable throne of his own? A great way to love, honor, and respect your husband as you decorate is to make "his chair" a priority. One of our first major furniture purchases was a hunter green leather recliner for Bill. Whenever he takes a moment to sit down, relax, and watch a football game or read the paper, it's always in his special chair. More and more manufacturers are creating updated, tasteful chairs that recline. These new styles are taking the once dreaded "recliner" to another level.

> Comfort, materials, and construction are as important as style.

PUT YOUR FEET UP

Saying, "Come on in! Put your feet up and stay awhile!" is a great way to make others feel at home in your home. Most ottomans are reasonably priced and come in all sizes and shapes — round, square, rectangular, tasseled, tufted, or ruffled. Ottomans serve various functions; they can provide additional seating, prop up tired legs, or hold trays or books. Putting casters on an ottoman adds even greater flexibility. For a twist on the traditional coffee table, cover a large ottoman in a durable fabric or leather.

TABLE TALK

Tables bring beauty, convenience, and comfort to your home. End tables, nightstands, and stacking tables all add versatility to any room and provide a perfect place for a beverage or book.

A game table or drop-leaf table can be a great multipurpose addition to your living area. Consider placing a drop-leaf or pub table behind your sofa to hold accessories and add interest. When you need a place to dine, just pull up a leaf.

For a custom coffee table, find an old dining table with character and cut down the legs. Our rectangular pine coffee table was a pub dining table when we stumbled on it in an old warehouse. We had the legs cut down and put a few coats of wax on it. It makes a perfect spot for books, beverages, and accessories. When we have a party or eat by the fire, we simply slip out the two side leaves and have a large surface to serve on.

Another option for a coffee table is to find an interesting base and top it with a heavy piece of beveled glass. A sturdy trunk also makes a handy surface and provides extra storage space for toys or blankets. When a client needed a fresh look for her living area but couldn't afford a new coffee table, she brought her tired wood coffee table back to life by simply painting it a happy blue. Being on a budget often inspires the most creative ideas!

A NATURAL LOOK

For visual interest and variety, look for accent furniture in natural finishes such as wrought iron, rattan, wicker, and bamboo. These pieces bring a bit of the outdoors indoors and add a touch of texture. Don't be afraid to mix them with other furniture styles.

> Versatility adds value to your furniture.

86

I love the casual elegance of bamboo. For the past several years, I have been on the lookout for a bamboo side table for our home. After pricing them at flea markets and antique shops, we came across just the right one at the right price in (of all places!) a fragrance store while on vacation in Highlands, North Carolina. We enjoy this special little accent piece as a new member of our furniture family. Already, I've had it in three cozy spots. No matter where it stands, it will always hold memories of our fall getaway. Educate yourself on fair furniture pricing by shopping — and always be on the lookout for beautiful bargains!

Simple Tips

Creating a Beautiful Bed

- Purchase a quality mattress and box spring set. Lie down on store samples to determine what firmness you need for comfortable sleeping.

- If comfort preferences differ, use two twin mattresses of desired firmness side by side on a king frame.

- If finances are limited, keep a pretty jar on your dresser to collect loose change to go towards your "beautiful bed frame" fund.

- Purchase a bed frame that suits your personal style.

- Place your bed in a spot where you have the greatest view.

- The most practical placement for a bed is in the middle of the longest wall.

- For a cozy look, consider angling your bed from a corner.

- For convenience and ease in making your bed, allow a minimum of 15" between the bed and wall.

- Assure your headboard is high enough to display pillows without being hidden. If there is a footboard, assure it doesn't block your view.

- Add texture and interest with beautiful, ready-made linens like a dust ruffle, coverlet, duvet comforter, quilts, shams, and assorted pillows. Many home decor stores and mail-order catalogs offer lovely, reasonably priced options.

- A bench at the end of your bed can hold pillows and folded bed coverings.

- Bunk beds, trundle beds, and daybeds maximize space and give sleeping flexibility to rooms (especially kids' rooms).

- A twin bed can be converted to a daybed by attaching a headboard on each end of the bed.

*A simple mix of color and texture makes the bed
in our master bedroom a favorite spot.*

Simple Tips

Choosing a Dining Table and Chairs

- Determine the size and shape of your table by your room size and the number of people you normally seat.

- Allow 18 inches per place setting on your tabletop.

- Allow 36 inches from the edge of your table to the wall for comfortable seating and accessibility.

- Round or oval tables are best for conversation and saving space.

- Square or rectangular tables are most suitable for multipurpose tables.

- Glass-top tables add light and visual space to a room and can show off an attractive table base or beautiful rug below.

- Table leg placement will affect seating capacity. A pedestal table provides for the most leg room.

- Pub tables, flip-top tables, drop-leaf tables, and tables with extra leaves provide the greatest flexibility for dining.

- If dining space is tight, create a corner booth or a window seat.

- Select your dining chairs based on comfort, size, and style.

- Standard chair seat height is 18 inches. Standard table height is 29–30 inches.

- Assure the apron (the wood piece under the tabletop) does not get in the way of legs.

- Unify two dining chairs of different styles by upholstering them in the same fabric.

- Vary matching chairs by recovering or slipcovering them with different fabrics.

- For comfort and coziness, put wing chairs in place of the usual end chairs.

- If using armchairs, measure the arm height to assure the arms will fit easily under tabletop.

Armless chairs upholstered in a practical green fabric
bring color and comfort to the maple kitchen table.

Simple Tips
Selecting a Sofa

- Standard sofa sizes are 60", 72", and 84".

- Measure your room to assure the sofa will fit comfortably.

- When selecting a sofa, consider your design options: Arm style? Back style? Skirt style? Exposed wood leg? Bun feet? Tight back? Loose pillow back? Any special detailing, like contrast welt cording, braided trim?

- Check for quality frame construction. Kiln-dried hardwood frame construction assures the sofa frame won't warp. Eight-way hand-tied construction gives long-lasting resiliency to sofa cushions.

- When possible, try it out. Do the sofa's dimensions support you and your family comfortably? What seat and back cushion construction do you prefer?

- When selecting a sofa fabric, keep in mind that the more textured and heavy a fabric is, the more durable.

- Cotton sofa slipcovers work great if you have children. They are durable, machine-washable, and have a casual, comfortable look.

- To confirm your fabric selection before ordering, obtain the largest sample possible of the fabric that you plan to use on the sofa. If necessary, purchase a yard of the fabric from the manufacturer.

- Consider using C.O.M.—customer's own material. This means you can cover the sofa in whatever fabric you provide. This treatment is more costly, but allows you to have a custom sofa.

- When ordering a sofa, designate if it will go on carpet or hard surface flooring, to assure the appropriate length sofa skirt.

A quality, comfortable sofa is the largest, most important upholstered piece for your home.

Simple Tips

Selecting Accent Furniture

- Search flea markets, junk shops, antique shops, and estate sales for beautiful bargains.

- Use an old linen press or armoire to house a television and stereo equipment or your computer. If it's not deep enough, cut a hole in the back or remove the back completely.

- Break up a matching set of furniture and let each piece's beauty stand on its own. Use a nightstand as a sofa end table. Try a bedroom dresser for a buffet service in the dining room.

- Determine which woods you like the most: pine, oak, maple, mahogany, cherry, or walnut. For an eclectic feel, tastefully mix a few finishes.

- For a new look, refinish an old piece of furniture and change the hardware.

- A skirted table is an economical way to add color and coziness to any room. Embellish a table skirt with cording, fringe, banding, or a ruffle. Or drape a lovely tablecloth, quilt, or blanket over the tabletop and puddle it at the floor. Top it off with a round piece of glass.

- For a unique, one-of-a-kind coffee table, find an old dining table with character and cut down the legs.

- For interest, bring a touch of natural texture indoors with wrought iron, wicker, rattan, or bamboo pieces.

Once a pub dining table, our pine coffee table is durable and functional.

Simply Windows

With the main building blocks of your furniture in place, it's time to think about your windows. The windows in your home are your eyes to the world. They come in all sizes, shapes, and styles. Though each lends its own architectural interest, the primary purpose of all windows is to bring inside the natural outside elements of light, beauty, and air.

The blessings of outside elements also bring challenges that require windows to be covered at times. Window treatments can control light or glare, provide privacy, and insulate. They can also hide an unattractive view, camouflage awkwardly shaped windows, or simply enhance a room's decor. Several factors can direct your window decorating decisions.

> Windows are the room's breath of life.
>
> **Julie Iovine**

TEMPORARY SOLUTIONS

Whenever possible, wait to dress your windows until you have lived in your home for awhile. If you need immediate privacy, install an inexpensive, temporary solution. Paper-pleated shades are very inexpensive, can be cut with scissors to fit your window, and stick inside your window frame with an easily removable adhesive strip. I encourage clients to use these when they first move into their homes and are focusing on other, more pressing decorating issues.

CHECK OUT YOUR CHOICES

Window treatments range from reasonably priced to extremely expensive. Cost will be determined by materials, labor involved, and installation. Prioritize your purchases. Focus on the rooms that need immediate attention. While saving to splurge on shutters, we lived in our current home for several years with most of the windows bare.

Let the sunshine in!

Shop around for good pricing and quality. Ask satisfied friends for recommendations. Custom window treatments will cost more, and many windows can be beautifully dressed with ready-made treatments. Home stores, decorating shops, and mail-order catalogs offer many simple solutions to making window treatments attractive and affordable. Check out your options.

WONDERFUL WINDOWS

Today's new houses have more windows and open floor plans. While this helps brighten and energize your home, it also adds cost if the windows need to be covered. If you live in a home with few windows, be sure the treatments you choose make the most of the light you have.

When you have a beautiful view, a simple, clean window with gleaming white trim may be all you need. When privacy is not necessary, consider letting a window's beauty and simplicity stand on its own. The more invisible your window seems, the more in touch you will feel with the outdoors.

If you need anything on your picturesque windows at all, approach your window treatment like a frame on a beautiful painting. Let it merely enhance your view, not distract it. Clients with a wonderful mountain view outside their picture windows occasionally needed privacy and sun protection. The simple decorating solution was to install a fabric cornice above the windows for softness, texture, and color. We then added pleated shades that could be dropped or pulled up and hidden completely beneath the top treatment.

When your window faces something unsightly or is extremely close to a neighbor's home, let its treatment distract your eyes from the view. The less desirable your window or view, the more dramatic you may want your treatment to be.

THE SUNNY SIDE

A room that faces east has its most direct light in the morning as the sun rises. If a room faces west, the strongest light will be in the early evening as the sun sets. Southern-exposed windows get the strongest, brightest light exposure dur-

> The windows in your home are your eyes to the world.

> The better the view, the less you need to do.

ing the day. This makes a room warmer and more cheerful, but also brings greater need to control light to reduce glare and fabric fading. Northern-exposed windows receive the least direct light, yet have the greatest need to be well insulated in the winter. Keep

your window exposure in mind when selecting fabrics or rugs for your rooms.

Every sunny day in my home office, the southeastern windows welcome the morning light as it streams in. I am drawn into this special place filled with warmth, sunshine, and energy. My office is one of my favorite rooms in our home, due largely to its window location and light patterns.

WHAT'S YOUR STYLE?

The possibilities for window treatment styles are as vast as clothing styles. Do you have a scheme yet for the room you are decorating? If you are unsure what style you want, refer to magazine clippings for ideas on window treatments.

My decorating style is simple and clean, so I prefer uncomplicated window treatments. For a classic and subtle look, I use white wood blinds or plantation shutters. For a casual, natural look, matchstick wood blinds are a perfect choice. For a soft, fresh feel, shirr lightweight curtains on a wood or iron rod. Perhaps your style is a bit more

Keep your window exposure in mind when selecting fabrics or rugs for your room.

99

elaborate or playful. Do you like trims and tassels? Do you like whimsical windows? However you treat your windows, be certain your selections work well with your room, your furniture, and your overall decorating style.

DECORATIVE TREATMENTS

There are basically two main types of window dressings: hard and soft treatments. Hard treatments tend to be more architectural and less decorative than soft treatments. When constructed of wood, they have a natural, classic look. When metal or man-made materials are used, they have a somewhat contemporary look. Shades, blinds, and shutters are examples of simple hard treatment solutions that provide light control, privacy, and decorative appeal.

Shades close from top to bottom and extend from casing to casing. Used alone or with top treatments, draperies, or curtains, they can be rolled up to enjoy a full view or rolled down for complete privacy.

Roller shades are one of the most economical options for windows and can be cut to size for mounting inside or outside window casings. Roller shades come in a choice of colors, textures, finishes, and privacy levels. They take up minimal space and can be raised or lowered with a simple pull.

Blinds are simply slats made of wood, metal, or vinyl that raise and lower with a cord and tilt to control light with a wand or cord. I like white, wood venetian blinds. They give a clean, simple look, while providing light and privacy.

Soft window treatments consist of any window dressings made out of fabric. Price range depends on fabric selection, the amount of fabric needed, materials, and labor costs. Soft treatments can be curtains, draperies, valances, and cornices. Curtains and draperies bring color, coziness, texture, and softness to a room. Curtains are casual and simply constructed. They are attached to a rod by ties, tabs, or pockets, and open and close by hand. Draperies are often lined and made of more elaborate fabrics, and tend to have more detailed construction and hardware.

When decorating a kitchen window that needed privacy on the lower half without sacrificing the sunlight, we used a white, cotton Battenburg lace curtain. We hung a café rod horizontally in the center of the window and shirred on the curtain. While the white cotton filtered the light and gave privacy, the sunshine still beamed in through the delicate cutwork of the lace fabric. The simple, beautiful treatment was easy and very economical.

Another popular top treatment for windows is a valance. Valances are made of fabric and come in a variety of styles. A cornice is a shallow, fabric-covered box that can be straight or shaped, and is mounted at the top of a window to conceal heading and hardware of other, more functional window treatments. Both top treatments are great solutions for children's rooms.

Curtains and draperies bring color, coziness, and texture to a room.

While working on a young boy's bedroom with a Western theme, we hung wood branches at the top of each window. We then took large, 54" squares of bandana-style fabric, folded them in half into triangles, and hung one over each branch, attaching the fabric to the branch with a sailor's knot on each end. The valance was simple, casual, inexpensive, and provided just the right look to enhance the little cowboy's windows.

CREATIVE CHOICES

In addition to the standard hard and soft treatments, creative options for enhancing windows abound. Beveled-glass windows, for example, provide privacy without blocking sunlight. This is a beautiful solution for a front door or a picture window over a large bathtub. In our tiny powder room, we have an old stained-glass window in place of an exterior window. This charming touch brings light, color, and beauty into the little room, while still allowing privacy.

If you have a bay window in your kitchen, why not turn it into a cozy window seat? It will maximize your kitchen size. Add hinges to the seat top to provide additional storage and load the seat with a fabric cushion and lots of pillows. The window seat will provide comfortable seating for your kitchen table and is a creative alternative that often proves no more costly than standard kitchen chairs.

Above all, remember, whatever you do with your windows, be sure you can still enjoy the greatest gift they can give your home — the light, beauty, and fresh air that only the outdoors can bring!

Simple Tips

Selecting Shades

- Customize shades with fabric or trim. For ease, try using a roller shade kit, found in most home decor stores. A custom shade combined with a fun top treatment is a cute choice for a child's bedroom.

- Pleated shades are made of thin, accordion-pleated fabric that compacts well when folded. They are available in a wide variety of fabrics.

- For a clean look that's more substantial than the pleated shade, consider a Roman shade. This tailored treatment can be custom-made in any fabric and has wide horizontal pleats that stack when drawn.

- Woven woods are shades made of natural fibers that look beautiful with most decorating styles. Matchstick wood shades are made of split bamboo and woven with string. Woven wood treatments give your windows style with economy. If backed with fabric, they are more room darkening.

- A balloon shade can be box-pleated for a tailored look that uses less fabric, or shirred with more fabric folds, for a feminine look.

- An Austrian shade is very shirred and puffy. In a beautiful, sheer fabric, this treatment looks elegant, and in a simple, cotton fabric, its feel is more casual and relaxed.

- For visual appeal and safety, install an attractive, brass cleat hook beside your window for wrapping any dangling cord when shades are pulled up.

The tortoiseshell Roman shade gives a natural, decorative look to windows.

Simple Tips

Selecting Blinds

- Wood blinds, with a header, are decorative and look attractive alone. Metal or vinyl blinds appear more functional and look best when used under curtains, draperies, or top treatments.

- Venetian blinds have two-inch slats made of wood, metal, or plastic, that are sometimes accented by thick cotton available in a variety of colors. The wood slats can be stained or painted.

- Venetian wood blinds are an economical alternative to plantation shutters (the cost of covering a window with a venetian wood blind is approximately one-half of that of a custom shutter), while providing a similar look from the exterior.

- Venetian blinds usually allow more light than shutters due to thinner slats and no wood framing.

- Similar in style to venetian blinds, mini-blinds have one-inch slats and micro-blinds have half-inch slats. Both are available in vinyl, aluminum, and wood, and in a variety of colors and stains.

The wood blinds gracefully filter the afternoon light in the sunroom.

Simple Tips

Selecting Shutters

- Shutters have a clean, uncluttered, and timeless look. They also bring dimension and architectural appeal to your windows.

- Though shutters are seemingly more costly than other treatments, no additional window dressing is necessary. The cost of shutters is comparable to custom fabric treatments.

- Shutters are visually appealing from the exterior and add value to your home.

- Shutters are available in wood or vinyl polymer. Wood shutters have a natural, authentic charm. Vinyl shutters are less expensive and will not peel or warp.

- Louvered shutters come in a variety of sizes and slat widths up to 3". They can be painted or stained to match wood trim.

- The wider the slats and the fewer the shutter panels per window, the greater the visibility and light.

- For simple installation, shutters can be mounted inside the window casing. For a more finished look, shutters can be mounted outside the window casing in a self-enclosed, wood frame.

- For flexibility, have two separate wood strips to control top and bottom shutter louvers. This allows for privacy on the lower half of the window, while letting in light on the upper half.

With shutter panels swung open, the window can be fully exposed to let in daylight.

simple Tips

Selecting Curtains and Draperies

- Make a window appear wider by using a longer rod and extending it beyond the width of the actual window frame.

- Visually heighten a room by using floor to ceiling draperies or curtains.

- For a reasonably priced designer window treatment, purchase ready-made curtains or draperies from home stores or mail-order catalogs. Hang them on iron or wood rods with decorative finials.

- For a soothing backdrop, use subtle neutral curtains or draperies. A simple, lace panel shirred on a wood rod is delicate and adds softness.

- For a dramatic statement, use bold, colorful fabrics.

- For an inexpensive, no-sew curtain, hang a pretty sheet by shirring a rod through the seamed pocket on the bottom or top of the sheet.

- Tablecloths make casual, reasonable curtains. Simply stitch a rod pocket along the appropriate edge and shirr onto a decorative rod.

- Café curtains cover the lower half of a window. For a functional and flexible treatment in casual settings, use tiered café curtains on windows, with one set of café curtains above another.

- For a casual, yet elegant look, allow stationary side panels to puddle on the floor.

- Lining protects your fabric from the sun, blocks light, gives body, and adds insulation. The most popular lining is a white or off-white cotton sateen. Blackout lining is a heavy, rubberlike fabric that completely blocks out light.

simple tie-top panels introduce the palette fabric in the main living area.

Simple Tips

Selecting a Valance or Cornice

- Make a window appear taller with a valance or cornice mounted above the actual window frame.

- Valances or cornices are simple window solutions for kids' rooms. They use minimal fabric and can be designed in endless, creative styles.

- For a finishing touch, use trims, tassels, fringes, or buttons to embellish simple top treatments.

- Create an easy awning or circus canopy by using two curtain rods with different returns. With a rod pocket at the top and bottom of your fabric, thread the shorter return rod through the top pocket and the longer return rod through the bottom.

- Use a wood branch, golf club, hockey stick, or anything fairly straight and unique as the pole for your window treatment. Fold a large square of fabric in half to make a triangle. Drape fabric over your rod and tie in knots at the corners.

- For a quick and easy soft swag, loosely thread fabric through two S-brackets mounted in the upper corners of your window.

- For a quick cornice, buy a ready-to-cover Styrofoam cornice board kit from a home decorating store.

A simple valanced window welcomes our back door guests.

simple Tips

Selecting Unique Window Solutions

- For privacy and light, enhance a special window or door with beveled or stained glass.

- Take advantage of the natural beauty of a ficus tree or other large, indoor plant to provide the privacy screen you need.

- Hang a bamboo pole across the top of your window. Create a naturally beautiful valance by using raffia to tie dried bunches of colorful flowers to the bamboo across the window.

- For a touch of outdoors, mount old, weathered, exterior shutters on both sides of an interior window.

- For simple interest and a splash of color, paint your window trim and other wood trim a bright contrast color.

- Enhance a window by hand-painting around it.

- For a charming, casual look, install a decorative plate rack above a kitchen window for accessories.

A cozy kitchen window seat provides seating and storage.

Simply Accessories

When it comes to decorating, accessories are the icing on the cake! Without them, rooms lack the best part — the part that gives your personal signature and reveals what you celebrate in life. Once the floors and walls are prepared, your major furniture pieces in place, and your windows treated, you're ready to add your favorite toppings, the accessories.

Accessories are any finishing touches that enhance a room — artwork, lighting, collections, framed photos, plates, books, and more. No matter where you live, affordable, attractive accessories are available that can take a basic home from boring to beautiful.

> Accessories are the icing on the cake!

SHOP IN YOUR OWN HOME

When accessorizing, first clear all of the existing accessories from the room and place them on a table. This will allow you to see your room with a fresh set of eyes. Then, open up your cabinets and drawers to see if you have some hidden treasures to display. Perhaps a lovely silver dish you received as a wedding gift can be polished and used to display a fragrant potpourri. Maybe a pretty crystal bowl can hold a scented candle. Or those dessert plates you seldom use could surround a mirror on your wall. Check other rooms to see if there are accessories that might be more suitable to the room you are accessorizing. Glance over the objects you had previously displayed in the room to see if anything should be used again. Only place objects in your room that are beautiful to your eye and functional for your needs. Store accessories you don't want to display for now, and give away those items that no longer appeal to you.

Select items that convey your passions.

When Bill and I married, we used a silver goblet that was a family heirloom for communion in our wedding service. Now we keep it as a special water glass in our guest bathroom. It's beautiful, functional, and holds significant life memories. Life is today! Enjoy your treasures while you live.

Don't overlook the family attic for discovering accessories, either. You may find special mementos to add a piece of family history to your home. Frame old black-and-white photos of relatives. Have a mirror cut for an antique frame. Make pillows from old table linens.

SHOP AROUND TOWN

In addition to hunting through your home, there are endless places to purchase unique accessories. Have fun looking at flea markets, garage sales, home decorating stores, discount stores, and antique shops. Avoid purchasing items just to fill up space. Instead, buy things you love, things that you could use in many spots in your home. Select items that convey your passions, beautiful books on topics that appeal to you, objects in pleasing colors, baskets in interesting textures, art that expresses your heart.

As with many things in life, I usually find my most treasured accessories when I least expect to. I may be shopping for something in a discount store and stumble upon a beautiful platter, a wonderful vase to transform into a lamp, or a whimsical birdcage. If I see an accessory I think a client will like, I snatch it up immediately. It can always be returned. Many of my favorite accessories have been found on a whim.

When possible, buy two of
the same accessory.

When possible, buy two of the same accessory. Two lamps, two urns, two plates. This gives you the flexibility to display them side by side or use them separately. In general, beautiful objects arranged symmetrically in pairs have a more traditional, balanced feel. Accessories displayed asymmetrically in odd numbers have a more contemporary and casual appeal.

For several years, I worked as an accessory buyer and visual display merchandiser for a large furniture store in Dallas. My job was to buy beautiful accessories like lamps, artwork, and artifacts and weave them into basic vignettes of furniture. Often, a whole room of furnishings would sell as soon as it was properly accessorized. The accessories gave the final touch that completed the room and helped customers visualize the furniture in their home.

CHARMING COLLECTIONS

If someone walked into your home when you were not there, what would they learn about you? What do your accessories say about you and your family? Begin a collection, if you don't have one. Discover something you love and make it a hobby to collect objects that reflect that passion: teapots, trophies, candleholders, clocks, copper, brass, books, boxes, pewter, pictures, pottery — anything that strikes your fancy.

One of my favorite things to collect are white serving platters. These crisp, clean platters are the perfect backdrop for displaying food when entertaining. The colors and textures of the food look beautiful against the smooth, white porcelain.

Another easy accessory to collect is beautiful books on a particular topic. Keep stacks on the coffee table, on side tables, and on bookshelves. Collected one by one, these bound pages can reflect your passion for a certain subject.

A timeless collection is blue-and-white porcelain pieces. You can find inexpensive pieces in discount home shops and pricey pieces in antique shops. Mixing the inexpensive objects with a few costly treasures gives the whole collection a priceless charm. The fresh contrast of these cobalt blue-and-white pieces will make any spot in your home bright and happy.

Have fun collecting picture frames. They are inexpensive accessories that can hold memories of the special people in your life. Display clusters of frames in your bedroom, living room, kitchen, and anywhere else looking for a spot of love and charm.

WHAT'S YOUR STYLE?

Is your decorating style one of cozy clutter, or is it clean and more sparse? The more you have on display, the more difficult to dust, and the harder it is to enjoy an item's simple beauty. Don't overdo when accessorizing. Too much clutter causes confusion and distracts your eyes from focusing on the beauty before you. Edit what you put out. Rearrange your accessories for interest. Put some away for a season. Keep things fresh.

Rather than having lots of miscellaneous accessories scattered randomly about your room, create visual impact with a few large objects or a collection of similar items clustered together. For a winter accessory, display a big basket of large pinecones on a coffee table. In the summer, replace it with a large glass bowl filled with jumbo seashells. If you don't feel confident with accessorizing your home, look to accessory arrangements in a favorite magazine clipping for inspiration.

Don't overdo when accessorizing.

A TOUCH OF HUMOR

Decorating is more fun if it's not taken too seriously. Try to have an accessory in every room that makes you smile, something that brings a touch of humor. A painting by a relative, a tiny pair of your child's first shoes, a framed photo of a funny memory. One wall in our home holds an old oil painting of Bill's grandfather and grandmother. The painting reminds him of their precious lives, but also makes any admirers chuckle and inquire about the dapper couple. His grandfather looks like he's scratching his ear and his grandmother has a large feather stemming from her hat. You can't look at the painting without cracking a smile!

LET THERE BE LIGHT

Light was the first element created by God, and he declared it as good! Yet most homes are light deficient. Many people don't have enough lighting fixtures in their homes, and the few they do have, they seldom turn on. One of the greatest and easiest ways to enhance your home is with good lighting. Light is energizing and welcoming. It sets the mood and affects our mood.

There are three basic types of lighting for your home. First, general lighting — chandeliers, ceiling or

> Light is energizing and welcoming.

> Let there be light.
>
> **Genesis 1:3**

wall-mounted fixtures, or recessed or track lighting — provides comfortable overall lighting. We recently installed four recessed ceiling lights — one in each corner of our home office — to lighten up the room. The difference is amazing! Once dark, the entire hunter green room is now bright and light.

The second type is task lighting, which focuses the light source on a specific task such as cooking, reading, homework, sewing, or computer work. Choices of task lighting are portable lamps, down-spots, track lighting, and recessed lighting. Each provides focused, bright light to prevent eyestrain. Lamps — available in all sizes, shapes, styles, and prices — are convenient sources for task lighting. I often encourage clients to have two down-spots installed over their bed, on separate switches. These provide great task lighting for reading in bed. Table lamps, floor lamps, and swing-arm lamps can all be found for reasonable prices in home decorating stores and mail-order magazines. Consider wiring an interesting object into a lamp and adding a decorative shade. Use a three-way lightbulb for various light levels and ambience. The brighter your light, the more enjoyable your task will be.

A third type of lighting is accent lighting. Accent lighting highlights an area or spotlights objects such as paintings, artwork, or plants. A simple, inexpensive can light shining upright in a corner works well for highlighting a plant and casting dramatic shadows on the walls. A picture light mounted above a painting can bring the colors in a painting to life. A standing torchère lamp can lend drama and accent an interesting ceiling or corner. Whatever you do to accessorize your home, turn on the lights! Each type of lighting adds interest, function, and appeal to your home.

Simple Tips
Selecting Lighting

- For a reasonably-priced, custom lamp, wire an interesting object into a lamp, such as a ceramic vase, a porcelain teapot, or a silver or brass candlestick. A lamp shop can wire and mount almost any object onto a base. Top your lamp with a pretty shade and finial.

- Update an old lamp with a new shade.

- Give a custom look to a shade by covering it with fabric or banding it with trim or fringe. Many lamp stores offer this service.

- For accent lighting and dramatic shadows, stand a torchère lamp in a room's corner or place an uplight on the floor behind a plant or folding screen.

- Add a finishing touch of interest to a table lamp with a decorative finial.

- To bring a painting to life, install a spotlight in the ceiling or attach a picture light to the artwork. To avoid a dangling cord, install a gem box behind the painting to plug the picture light into.

- Use track or recessed lighting in the ceiling to highlight specific areas.

- Swing-arm lamps provide flexibility in lighting without occupying table or floor surface.

- Assure you have proper lighting beside your bed, chair, or sofa. To avoid glare, the light source should come from behind the shoulders. The bottom of the lamp shade should be at eye level, usually 40–42" from the floor.

- Use a three-way lightbulb in lamps used for task lighting.

- To easily alter the ambience of any room, install dimmers on all overhead lighting.

This friendly bunny was bought for a bargain and wired into a lamp.

simple Tips

Displaying Artwork and Mirrors

- Hang only what you love or what has sentimental value.

- A picture's frame should enhance, not dominate or distract from, your artwork. Oil paintings don't always need a frame.

- When selecting artwork, balance the visual weight, color, and scale of the artwork with nearby furnishings.

- Fill a hallway or stairway wall with framed photographs of family. Write on the back of the frame the names of those in the photograph and the year it was taken.

- Most artwork is hung too high. Hang artwork in relation to the furnishings in the room. For example, hang a piece over a sofa or chest about three inches above the top of the furniture. If your ceiling is high and you need to draw the eye up, top artwork or a mirror with an interesting artifact.

- Before hanging a collage of artwork, arrange it on the floor. Begin with the largest piece and build around it. Once arranged, hang your artwork on the wall in a similar pattern.

- For a casual, flexible feel, prop artwork on a mantel rather than hanging it on the wall.

- Have a beveled glass mirror cut for an old frame.

- For instant impact, collect a variety of small, interesting mirrors from flea markets and assemble them into a collage on a wall.

- Hang framed botanical prints, children's artwork, maps, sheet music, architectural drawings—anything that expresses your passions.

This collage of treasures reveals a passion for golf.

Simple Tips

Creating Collections

- Make it a fun hobby to collect a particular type of object that appeals to you.

- When accessorizing the top of any table with a collection, think of it as an empty canvas on which you apply colors, shapes, and textures. Put low objects towards the front and tall ones towards the back.

- Collect pretty frames and fill them with the faces of those you love. Candid, casual pictures are more friendly and real-life than posed portraits.

- To visually unite picture frames, select those made at least partially from the same material.

- Use baskets of all sizes and shapes to organize and decorate your home. Adorn the top of kitchen cabinets or refrigerator with baskets. Stack them under a table.

- For a touch of charm, collect and display decorative plates. Prop them on plate stands, or hang them with a wire plate hanger or on plate racks.

These blue-and-white porcelain pieces — or any collection — have more visual impact when displayed together.

PEPIN

SWEET SIMPLICITY

CHARLOTTE MOSS   A PASSION FOR DE...

A Roomful of Flowers

SIGNATURE STY...

TRADITIONAL HOME

interior inspirations

COLEFAX AND FOWLER

Simple Tips

Displaying Books

- Collect books on subjects that appeal to your interests. The book titles that fill your home should tell your family's life story.

- Use a short stack of books as a pedestal to raise objects such as a small lamp, clock, or picture frame.

- For interest, paint a contrasting color on the back of your bookshelves. Test the color on a piece of foamboard and slip it behind the bookshelf to assure you like it.

- To arrange bookshelves, clear everything off. Stagger books to the left on one shelf, then to the right on the next shelf. Fill in the blank spots with decorative accessories.

- Place all hardback books together, removing paper jackets and pulling spines flush to the edge.

- Stack large books horizontally on your shelves.

- Place a pretty book on a plate stand, letting its cover face forward.

- Transform homely hardback books into instant antiques by sponging on several coats of brown shoe polish or brushing on a wood stain finish.

- For a unique and dramatic look, fill your shelves with interesting objects other than books—all baskets, all colored glass, all wooden artifacts, all hats—whatever expresses your style.

Beautiful books on favorite topics make a delightful display for the coffee table.

A Simply "SenseSational" Home

Step by step, we've talked about simply decorating your home. We have discussed simple solutions for bringing beauty into your private world. We've rolled out the rugs, covered the walls, placed the furniture, treated the windows, and added the accessories. So what more could there possibly be?

A "SENSE" OF HOME

It's time to give your house a "sense" of home. In my previous books, *Creating A SenseSational Home*, *505 Quick Tips to Make Your Home SenseSational*, and *Simply SenseSational Christmas*, I discuss the fact that there's more to making a home than just pleasing the eye. Beauty matters immensely; it attracts and inspires. But for a simply "SenseSational" home, we need to arouse all of the five senses to create a balanced atmosphere full of life and love.

The finishing "SenseSational" touches are fun and easy to do, and are the most revealing element of your decorating. The ways you stimulate the senses in your home convey your passions. A bowl of shiny, green

Seeking beauty alone in our homes is hollow.

apples on your foyer table shows a love for God's creation and a desire for simplicity. A crackling, wood-burning fire in your fireplace reveals that you treasure coziness and warmth. A flickering, fragrant candle by the back door provides a friendly welcome. The sweet smell of goodies baking in the oven communicates love and care. The peaceful music on the stereo creates a sense of calm. A familiar needlepoint pillow tucked into the arm of a favorite chair brings a touch of comfort. A sweet-smelling blossom in a bud vase beside your bed brings beauty, fragrance, and life into your most private refuge. These simples gestures stir the senses, transforming a beautifully decorated but lifeless house into a warm and welcoming home.

Simple Tips
Fragrancing Your Home

- Bring life and beauty into a favorite spot in your home with fresh, fragrant flowers. Fill a terra-cotta pot or simple vase with sweet-smelling flowers like gardenia, paper-white narcissus, lilac, roses, freesia, or lily of the valley. For the most alluring fragrance, select white flowers. Refrigerate the flowers at night to preserve them longer.

- For a fragrant luxury, fill a pretty dish in your powder room with small, scented soaps in pleasing shapes.

- To preserve your wood furniture and give your home a clean, citrus smell, dust with lemon-scented furniture polish and clean, cotton cloths.

- Use scented candles in all sizes, shapes, colors, and fragrances to instantly give your home a sense of calm. Place one by your back door to welcome others home, or in your bedroom for a romantic evening. Put one beside the tub for a blissful bath, on your desk to bring pleasure to paperwork, or on your dining table for a peaceful meal.

- Display a few of your favorite perfumes on a silver tray on your bedroom dresser.

- Keep a small perfume bottle in a basket by the back door for a quick spray before greeting loved ones. They will love coming home!

- Place a lamp ring on a lamp's lightbulb in your foyer. Add several drops of a fragrant oil and turn the light on. Enjoy the fragrance as it fills your rooms and lasts for hours.

- For an instantly clean-smelling home before guests arrive, spray your kitchen sink with a cleanser, sponge it clean, and rinse. Visitors will think your whole home is spotless.

- Pull on the heartstrings of loved ones by popping something easy and delicious-smelling in the oven. Bake a big batch of fudge brownies or a dozen "slice and bake" cookies.

A simple vase casually filled with fresh
stock brings God's beauty and fragrance indoors.

Simple Tips

Enjoying Good Tastes at Home

- Use fresh fruit or vegetables to create beautiful accessories. Try squash and small pumpkins in the fall; green or red apples in the winter; lemons and limes in the spring; peaches, plums, and pears in the summer. The beauty and color of fresh fruits and vegetables will far outlast fresh-cut flowers, as well as provide nutritious, delicious foods to eat.

- Fill a pretty candy jar with special sweets that coordinate with your decorating color scheme.

- Treat yourself to the simple and satisfying ritual of taking time out of your day for a hot cup of tea. Sit in a favorite, sunny spot of your home and savor a moment of stillness as you sip.

- Tantalize taste buds by serving food beautifully. For an appealing meal, vary color, texture, and taste. For a pretty salad presentation, rather than tossing everything together, lay greens on a plate and layer ingredients. Then drizzle on a delicious dressing.

- Vary the room settings where you eat. Enjoy dinner by a cozy fire in the living room, breakfast on the patio on a sunny morning, or a late-night snack in bed.

Fresh, sweet pears tossed in a basket instantly create a beautiful centerpiece.

Simple Tips

Bringing Pleasant Sounds into Your Home

- For a welcoming jingle, tie a beautiful bell or strip of bells to your entrance doorknob.

- Enhance your home atmosphere with pleasing music. An excellent sound system will enhance the music quality. Wire speakers into adjoining rooms so you can experience great sound throughout your home.

- For a quiet home, select furniture, fabrics, and finishes that absorb sound. Upholstered furniture and lined fabric draperies enhance quietness. Carpet is the best sound absorber for floors, but wood floors absorb more noise than vinyl, tile, or stone. Paneling or upholstery on walls will also reduce noise.

- Open up your bedroom windows and listen to the sounds of nature. Let the peaceful sound of rain soothe you to sleep and the sweet sound of birds singing be your wake-up call.

- Begin a collection of pretty handbells. Mix old treasures found at flea markets or antique shops with new ones. Display your beautiful bells in a little spot looking for a touch of charming sound.

- Designate a special "get well" bell for sick family members to place at their bedside and ring when they need assistance.

- Enjoy the sweet chirp of a canary in your home. House your bird in a decorative birdcage and let her song become a part of your home's familiar sounds.

This treasured clock with its pleasant-sounding chimes rings "home" each time it strikes.

simple Tips

Bringing Comfortable Touches to Your Home

- Use pillows of all sizes, shapes, colors, and fabrics to personalize any upholstered furniture or bed. Add tassels, trim, cording, and buttons for interest and texture.

- Floor pillows provide great flexible seating or support for someone to plop on the floor to watch a movie. Stack two or three in your living room, playroom, or kids' rooms. Floor pillows create inexpensive seating and, with zippered covers, can be easily cleaned.

- Transform a door or cabinet by replacing its hardware with beautiful, functional knobs or handles that feel wonderful to your grasp.

- Roll up plush, terry-cloth towels and put them in a pretty basket by your bathtub. Fill another basket with your favorite touches like soaps, bath salts, lotions, powders, sponges, and brushes for a wonderful, luxurious bath.

- Envelope your mattress in bedsheets that are beautiful, comfortable, and suitable to your personal touch. Try cool, all-cotton sheets in the summer and cozy, flannel sheets in the winter.

- Cover your bed with the delightful look and feel of a down duvet. A duvet (meaning "fluff") is cool in the summer and warm in the winter and makes bed-making a breeze. With no top sheet or heavy blankets to wrestle, all you do is fluff and smooth your duvet. Purchase or make a duvet cover that coordinates with your bedroom decorating scheme.

- Use a silver toast caddy, brass letter rack, or basket for displaying paperwork on your desk that needs attention. Keep an attractive letter opener on hand to open your mail.

- Fill your home with a variety of textured elements: a woven sisal rug, a smooth glass-top table, an iron drapery rod, or a handmade piece of pottery.

- Create a cozy corner in your bedroom where you can sit, read, and enjoy a morning cup of coffee or a late-night cup of tea. Try a love seat and ottoman, or a chaise lounge and small side table.

This chenille chair and cozy throw invites any passerby to curl up and stay awhile.

For more information on SenseSational Homes or Terry Willits, write:

SenseSational Homes, Inc.
P.O. Box 70353
Marietta, GA 30007

Call 1–800–891–3116 or visit our website at www.sensesationalhomes.com.